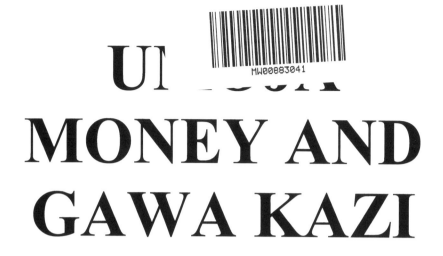

UMOJA MONEY AND GAWA KAZI

Beyond "Buy Black": A System for Building Community and Social Capital

Maaskelah Kimit Thomas, PhD

Umoja Money And Gawa Kazi
Beyond "Buy Black": A System for Building Community and Social
Capital
Copyright © 2011 by Maaskelah K. Thomas PhD
Published by Transformative Concepts
Wichita, Kansas 67214
www.transformativeconcepts.com

Printed in the United States of America

"Return to the way, the way of reciprocity. Not merely taking, not merely offering. Giving, but only to those from whom we receive in equal measure. Receiving, but only from those whom we give in equal measure. How easy, how just the way. Yet how easily, how utterly you have forgotten it." - Ayi Kwei Armah

INTRODUCTION

First, let me paint a brief scenario.

Sheila, a student, is on a limited budget, but a special project she's working on for a class this semester requires that she make tons of copies. Whereas a few copies might be manageable, lately she's been spending well over $20 a week, running back and forth to the copy shop. She has her own PC, and is a skilled typist. She discovers that Greg, a young attorney with a new, independent practice, accepts UMOJA Money for various things, so she approaches him about using his copier and paper, in exchange for the local currency. They transact.

Greg, struggling to set up his new office, discovers that he really needs some shelves for his growing law library. He turns to Asante, a presently "unemployed" young brother who learned carpentry while incarcerated for three years. His work is good, and although he has been unable to find employment, those in the community who know of his work utilize his services on occasion. Greg contacts him and Asante is willing to accept UMOJA Money. They transact. With the money he saved in the transaction, Greg was able to hire an enterprising youth, on an as-needed basis, to maintain the lawn outside his small office for the summer.

In the meantime, Imani, a young single mother on welfare with two small children, finds that, try as she might, her food stamps just don't last throughout the whole month. Although she stretches them as far as she can, the end of the month is always sparse. However, she has been doing some babysitting in her home for two other single mothers who are currently in trade school, attempting to better their lives. In payment from one, she receives UMOJA money. For the last several months, she has been transacting with Herman, a middle-aged speech pathologist who does gardening more for a hobby than anything. He calls it his therapy. He is good at it, though, and always produces much more than he and his family could every use. So, he provides fresh vegetables to supplement Imani's food requirement, and she pays him with UMOJA money.

BATTER AND COMMUNITY MONEY
(UMOJA Money)

The Oxford Dictionary defines a barter exchange as a method or system by which debits and credits in different places are settled, or by which goods and services are exchanged without the actual transfer of money. Bartering and trading are the oldest form of commerce known to man, and is in fact the basis of any economic system. In a pure barter system, I provide you with something you need or value in exchange for something that I need or value. It's as simple as that. The evolution of that system has grown into a world economy and that economy is no longer controlled by its user, but is controlled by a small group of international bankers and financiers who not only control the value of that exchange (which has become considerably more "sophisticated"), but who also control who has access to it at whatever level. This may not be bad, in and of itself, but when something of such importance to many is controlled by a relative few, it may be important for the many to be able to assess the accountability of that few. In the case of the current western and European monetary environment, that is not (nor has it ever been) the case.

Nevertheless, bartering is still practiced, even at the national and international corporate level: nearly 40% of Fortune 500 companies utilize barter in some form or another, especially those seeking new avenues for expansion and profit. Increasingly, businesses large and small are turning to trade as a means to increase sales to new customers, conserve their cash outlays, and to increase their bottom line. But it is not only businesses that benefit; the entire community can be uplifted as result, if a community develops a comprehensive plan to identify, utilize and maximize its internal resources.

You may ask, why the need for a physical currency, as opposed to just a barter and trade situation? One very good, and obvious, reason is that in a barter/trade situation, one person has to have what the other person needs, and vice versa, for the transaction to happen.

For example: Marjorie, a community elder, makes beautiful crocheted baby sweaters and sells them to local consignment shops and small outlet stores. However, she'd like to learn more about the Internet, to explore the possibilities of marketing her wares to a wider market. Tariq is skilled at Internet marketing, and occasionally creates websites for others. Marjorie definitely could benefit from instruction from Tariq, but Tariq has absolutely no need for baby sweaters. Marjorie could pay him a fee to teach her, but her cash is limited. Nevertheless, a barter transaction is not feasible in this situation. With a physical medium of exchange, mutually agreed upon by all, an exchange is possible.

In fact, this is the basis of the western monetary system. Let's take a little walk back in history and look at that and see what went wrong.

WHAT'S IT WORTH?

Paper money, as we know it, began as "promissory notes," a note written on a piece of paper promising to repay a debt. Using the above example: say Tariq has no need for sweater, but he thinks his sister may be pregnant and he may want to purchase some later. Marjorie writes him a "note" so that at some later date, he can come and get the value in the goods she provides. As it turns out, Tariq's sister isn't pregnant, but he has a good friend with a newborn who also designs software. In exchange for a software program his friend provides, Tariq gives him Marjorie's promissory note for three handmade baby sweaters. The friend delivers the note back to Marjorie, who proceeds to produce and deliver the sweater. True barter.

However, what happens if Marjorie, thinking that Tariq probably won't redeem the note in the near future, also promises several other sweaters to other people --- more than she currently has the time or materials to produce. And what if everybody comes at the same time to redeem their promissory notes, and Marjorie can't produce? To alleviate the situation, Marjorie arbitrarily decides to charge twice as much for each sweater, thus potentially decreasing the demand and the number of sweaters she's called upon to produce --- AND garnering some additional profit from the deal. This is called inflation.

With the US dollar, the commodity that was originally promised was gold. Paper money was originally based on the gold standard. Small bankers and lenders were called upon to safe keep the gold of others, for which they also set and/or negotiated the value. As a receipt for the deposit, the owners of the gold were given paper notes. The owners could then pass the paper notes in exchange for goods and services, as opposed to walking around with bags of gold for commerce and trade. The paper notes circulated, "as good as gold," and most who used and received the notes rarely came to collect the actual physical gold. After all, they knew it was there in the safe, should they ever need it, and the paper money was infinitely more convenient and easier to transport. The safe keepers, on the other hand, found that it was profitable to "lend" promissory notes to others based on the value of the gold they were safekeeping. Since most of the owners of the gold never actually came to collect the actual ore, but instead passed the paper promises, they felt secure that they would be able to cover any requests for redemption that did come in. In addition, they charged interest to the borrowers, and thus were able to make a profit from gold that didn't even belong to them. The problem was that for each sack of gold that may have originally been worth, say, $1 million, the lenders had now given out $4 million worth of promises on it. This was fine, as long as no more than $1 million worth of requests for redemption came in at one time. But if they did, the lender had the option to arbitrarily reduce the value of the gold; thus a promise of $50,000 might now only be worth $30,000, and the holder of the note would have to take less than he was originally promised, or produce more notes than were originally agreed upon for the same amount of gold. This is a simple description of inflation. However, as long as the demand never exceeded the amount in holding, the lenders (the creators of both value and the paper money representing that value) stood to make great profit, basically because they were creating something (paper currency) out of nothing, and profiting from the indebtedness of others (via interest). The borrowers, on the other hand, found themselves struggling and toiling to repay a debt of arbitrary value to begin with. (Sound familiar?) What was originally created to assist the system of barter and exchange has ultimately created domination and control by the small group who has the power to create the money.

Incidentally, out of that paper money system developed the concept of "central banks," and subsequently, the establishment of our own FEDERAL RESERVE BANK, which creates, distributes and sets the value on what we now call money. Most people are not aware that the Federal Reserve Bank is NOT a federally-owned agency, but is, in reality, a privately-owned bank, over whose direction we (the American people) have no control. Its leaders are not elected, but rather, are appointed by our government; and once appointed, our government has no direct control over their decisions and actions. Don't you ever wonder about the multi-trillion dollar Federal debt, and to whom this great, wealthy nation owes multiple trillions of dollars? Our current economic crisis is making that more abundantly clear, although I encourage you to do more research on that topic.

COMMUNITY CURRENCY

What is money but a means of exchange? Yet, communities and even nations suffer from a shortage of money. Money within our community generally comes in from outside of the community and rushes right back out, without providing any internal nurturance or growth, other than to the particular individual who used it. When the amount of money circulating within our community falls, due to unemployment (currently at close to 25%) or changes in government spending (budget cutting of social services and safety net programs), so does the level of trading within the community, if there ever was any. Businesses decline, people lose jobs, some businesses fail. There is a "shortage of money." But what is money but a means of exchange? The paper currencies we pass between us have no value in and of itself --- try eating it or building a house out of it.

Money is simply a measure of value. And there can never be a shortage of a measure. Imagine running out of inches or miles. So, what we view as a "shortage of money" is really just the lack of a viable means of exchanging value for value. The materials for building the house are there, along with the skills necessary to build it; the vegetables are growing in the garden, the computer is up and running; the fabric is there for the dress. The problem is not the lack of goods and services, but the means to set a value and method of exchange, so that those who need them can acquire them at a reasonable and relative exchange value.

Community currency is one means of designing an internal, community controlled system of exchange. Community currencies, or local currencies, are not a new concept, but the utilization of them is experiencing a major resurgence throughout the world. Such internal currency systems provide a tool for addressing issues such as unemployment, and community breakdown and disenfranchisement. Some other benefits of community currencies include:

- Individuals and the communities in which they reside regain control over the economic decision-making that affects their neighborhood/local community.

- The community is able to safely and simply increase the money supply in the community without causing inflation.

- The community is able to separate the contradictory functions of money, e.g. as a store of value on external markets versus a medium of exchange at the community level.

- Money/currency has an opportunity to circulate and build WITHIN the community, instead of always going outward, thus enhancing local production capabilities in the community in order to meet of human needs and create security relative to the community's basic needs.

- The community is able to identify and effectively utilize individual and community assets to meet the needs of the community.

- The community is able to support reduction, reuse and recycling of goods.

- The community increases the options for its members to stay and work in their community and not have to journey to other places to earn money.

- Human security --- social, economic, cultural --- is increased.

- Local/community self-reliance and the community's ability to weather an economic downturn or crisis, and to insulate itself and its less advantaged members are increased.

- The quality of life in a community, social harmony, mutual aid, cooperation and reciprocation are positively impacted.

- The community is able to look beyond economic valuation, to consider social and environmental values and impacts.

- The local community is increasingly able to provide a means for employment for displaced or marginal workers, people in transition, or trying out new fields.

- Individuals within the community are encouraged to contribute to their community in ways that improve the entire community.

- Local currency systems help to provide economic, as well as political, enfranchisement and choice, especially for those who are poor and often offered few choices.

- Community members are able to view resources from a renewed perspective that acknowledges that there really is enough for everyone, if everyone shares, and that there is no need to compete for resources or to meet one's basic needs.

- Social capital becomes more important and valuable than material capital.

- Both the individual and collective sense of self-esteem and self-worth and pride in the community & culture increases, and cultural and historical pride is increased as well.

Several systems have been established around the country that are providing practical success for the communities involved. Systems like the LETS system (see http://www.gmlets.u-net.com/), utilized in several communities around the country, and Ithaca Hours, in Ithaca New York (see http://www.ithacahours.org/) are providing the means for communities to service their own needs from within, provide financial boosts for businesses, provide creative work opportunities for residents, and develop genuine unity and shared work within communities. The key element to success is the ability to link unused or underused resources to otherwise unmet needs. For us in the African American community, the key is to develop means and methods to utilize such a system within our local communities, and ultimately, even across national and international trade systems.

So, the logical next question is: how does it work? Before we go there, I want to give you some examples and testimonials of how such a system can and does work. These are real examples from the Ithaca, New York community.

- ✓ Dan (has received local currency for his deli goods and has used local currency to purchase everything from Christmas presents to chiropractic care): "With this system, money doesn't head north, south, east or west. It creates our own mini-economy."
    - ✓ Margaret (has received local currency for rent payment and for phone calls, has used local currency for food, movies, engineering consulting, books and gifts): "Because [local currency] can be used both for goods and services which are not always part of the formal economy and for retail and professional transactions, the local economy gets a boost every time it's earned. That's what any money is all about --- facilitating exchanges among people."
    - ✓ Barbara (sells and repairs shoes, and accepts local currency; has purchased gifts and advertising): "This is really starting to take off. I wouldn't

have bought gifts where I did, except that they [accepted the local currency]. This money makes everybody more aware of what's valuable in the community. So it helps community development by keeping money local."

✓ Ramsey (sells bagels at the local bakery and has bought landscaping, meals, printing, air conditioning consulting, eyeglasses and groceries): "[Local money] keeps people in our community employed better than dollars that leave the community. Dollars that go to large corporations do not really trickle back down, they concentrate capital, making the rich richer and the poor poorer. We see America's inner cities becoming Third World countries as a result. What's better about [local currency] is that since you can't bank them, you have to spend them to benefit, so you don't get the concentration of capital."

✓ Rabbi Eli (offers Hebrew lessons and Bar/Bat Mitzvah lessons): "The barter list has been very useful. Recently, I traded lessons for violin repair. [Local currency is] a very creative support network, a good model for preserving kindness and compassion in the economy. They avoid the mass business focus and remind us that we're serving other human beings."

The stories and testimonials from members of this community go on and on. Exchanging everything from computer sales and service to childcare and housing, communities around the world have discovered ways to better utilize their own resources to meet local needs, while at the same time, building and strengthening each other and the community.

There are some things that need to be assessed about a community to determine the feasibility of community bartering, exchange or cooperative system. Each community is different, and has to be considered in its uniqueness. However, there are some priority conditions that can make community currency most feasible. These include issues related to:

- The *economic condition* of the community (What are the physical attributes of the community? Are there any/many home-based businesses? Are there a variety of goods and services available for sale/trade and what is the capacity, e.g. supply vs. demand?)
- The *social conditions* of the community (Are community members motivated to improve community conditions? What types of leaders are available and involved in the community, e.g. are they honest, helpful, focused on the good of the community and willing/eager to share leadership with the community in a participatory fashion?)
- The *political landscape* of the community (Would the local political leadership – municipal, state, etc. --- be open to support community-based currency and/or trade activities? What might be some of the political obstacles?)
- *Community culture* (Do neighbors know and reach out to each other? Is sharing and assistance a community value within the area? Do neighbors/residents regularly assist and serve each other, when opportunities arise? Are there organizations, whether formal or informal, that regularly provide opportunities for community residents to assist each other?)
- *Geography* (What is the geographical location of your identified community? Is it rural or urban? Is it isolated or well integrated into the larger community? Are there clear boundaries?)
- *Human capital/resources* (Are there community members who with skills in a variety of areas needed

for the development and sustainability of this kind of project, e.g. bookkeeping/accounting, organizational management, clerical, etc., or are there organizations within the community which might partner in such an initiative? How are community programs and organizations regarded by community members? What part does religion/spirituality play in the life of the community, and how might that enrich an effort like this?)

The how to? For our communities, it is a matter of developing local currency systems that work for us. However, there are a variety of systems to consider.

Time Banking, also known as a Service Exchange, is a reciprocal service exchange in which TIME is considered the currency. The unit of currency is valued at an hour's worth of any person's labor, and is often referred to as Time Dollars. Time Banking is most valuable for its re-valuing of services that are often devalued in a money market system, things such as child- or elder-care, mentoring, housekeeping, or light clerical duties. Time spent providing services such as these, but certainly not limited to these, earns the person providing the service Time Dollars which can be spent on other services. The beauty and value of Time Banking is that it can increase interaction between neighbors and community members who might otherwise not have engaged with each other. The core values of Time Banking are:

- Everyone is an asset
- Some work is beyond a monetary price
- Reciprocity in helping
- Social networks are necessary
- A respect for all human beings

Local Exchange Trading Systems (LETS) also known as LET Systems are locally initiated, democratically organized, not-for-profit community enterprises that provide a community information service and record transactions of members exchanging goods and services by using the currency of locally created LETS Credits. LETS, unlike direct barter, is a fully fledged monetary or exchange system. Members of LETS networks earn credits from any member and spend them with anyone else within the network. Each network works out their own system, making it unique and beneficial for all within the system, but some basic principles include:

1. Local people set up an organization to trade between themselves, often paying a small membership fee to cover administration costs

2. Members maintain a directory of offers and wants/needs to help facilitate trades

3. Upon trading, members may 'pay' each other with printed notes, log the transaction in log books or online, or write checks which are later cleared by the system accountant.

4. Members whose balances exceed specified limits (positive or negative) are obliged to move their balance back towards zero by spending or earning.

For our purposes, I am recommended a system that is a hybrid of the aforementioned systems. I will outline some of the basic requirements for developing and initiating such a system within a community. I am calling this system UMOJA (the Swahili word for Unity), and the currency, UMOJA Money. Although the system necessarily is a local community system, it can be developed to expand into other communities, thereby setting up an even larger network of likeminded individuals and collectives. But for now, let's start on your block:

The potential for utilizing a community currency is only limited to the knowledge, skills, goods and services available within any community and the willingness among the residents to share them for the common good of all.

The benefit is that the currency (thus, the value of the goods, services, etc.) remains within the network, while freeing up hard cash for goods, services, knowledge and skills that may not yet be obtainable within the network, or which are only available through the use of hard cash. And where established businesses are involved, it allows more readily available cash flow to "grow the business," thus enhancing the possibility of providing valuable employment opportunities for others in the community.

Another less tangible benefit is the sense of community unity (UMOJA) and working together (HARAMBEE) that such a system engenders. In the scenario presented, every person involved can feel a sense of having assisted another human being (not a multinational corporation) to improve their lives, if only in small ways.

So, just what does to take to create and establish such a system? (This is the good part. You won't believe how simple it really is!)

CREATING A COMMUNITY CURRENCY SYSTEM

Most of the elements necessary to make a community currency system possible are already in place in many African American communities. There are only five key elements required.

1. A progressive, community-minded, organized group of individuals to put the rest of the elements together into a format workable within their own community. (Is that you?)
2. An "exchange listing." This can be a community newsletter, website or blog, designed specifically for this purpose or, if a community newspaper is currently in publication, a page of the local paper can be utilized for the same purpose. Some communities even have local directories of black-owned businesses, whose publishers would surely revel at the idea of such a cooperative network!
3. Individuals and businesses that will agree to exchange goods, services, knowledge and skills as part of such a network, and will accept payment, even if only in part, in the local currency. With businesses, this may or may not be the good and/or services which constitute the primary activity of the business. (For tax purposes, local currency received by an established business for goods or services that do NOT constitute their "regular" business earnings – remember the earlier example of Sheila and the copies? – is tax-free. When in question, consult a tax professional.)
4. A local currency, meaning the actual physical item. You (meaning the group who sets up the system) design this yourself. I have included a rough example of what that might look like, but the design is entirely up to you. If possible, create the design with some unique feature that makes it hard to

duplicate (although a key element of the system is the integrity of the people involved). One community prints their money on a special, handmade paper stock produced locally, which contains a unique watermark. There are several paper mills that produce special watermarked paper that could likewise be used. Find one that works for you, or find some other means to "mark" your money to decrease the possibility of fraud. Additionally, if there is a graphic artist in the community, they might be commissioned to design the "dollar bill" and may be the first one to receive an issue, as payment.

5. Community involvement. It is ideal if a group of community members --- even if it's only four or five – are involved in the initial development of the system. Each of those individuals would agree to exchange whatever good or services they have to offer for the local currency, even if only between each other. Others who agree to use the currency are brought into the network gradually. When others see that the system works, and can potentially meet some of their needs, they will at least be willing to try it. And because no actual money is vested, all they risk is their time and their skills, and they stand to gain the opportunity to help themselves and to assist another human being toward independence and self-determination.

The implementation of the system is equally as simple. Basically, all those who agree to exchange the community currency are given an initial issue, along with a listing of business, goods and services where they might be exchanged. The amount of the initial issue is up to those initiating the system, but will probably be based around the goods and services available at that time, and what is reasonable to encourage that participants pass the currency. In Ithaca, each new entity is given two (2) Ithaca Hours, equal to $20, in whatever denominations they choose. From there, they are free to use the currency within the system as they choose. If a party not currently listed as part of the network agrees to accept the currency, they are also free to use it within the system (and hopefully will decide and agree to become an official member of the network). "Membership" in the network requires no special obligation, other than an agreement to accept and use the currency where possible. There need be no "dues" or mandatory meetings or any other organizational type activities for network members, unless those in the network deem it necessary and appropriate. Some community currency systems requirement nominal annual membership dues to offset the expenses of printing the currency, updated the network listings and overall promotion of the network. One community who uses a community currency system hosts periodic potlucks, where members come together to assess the system, to get to know one another, and to work out any kinks in the system. This is probably a good idea, if for no other reason than the development of a sense of community mission. Nevertheless, that is entirely up to each community.

Additional currency can be created as needed. The increased money supply will not create "inflation." On the contrary, because community currency is designed to link unused/underused resources with otherwise unmet needs, an increase in the currency can have a "booster" effect, inspiring users to look for additional uses and applications. And because the currency can only be used within the network, there is not benefit from hoarding it. Thus, its free flow continues to recycle resources throughout the system.

So, there you have it. There may be those who question the premise of going "beyond buy black." Those who do may have missed the point.

(Excuse me while I climb atop my soapbox):

While it is certainly true that our community is in need of economic development and uplift, money (hard cash) is not the only vehicle toward that end. Human capital is one of the most valuable resources on earth. And "what does it profit a man to gain the whole world and lose his soul?" No matter the challenges that continue to press against us due to institutional racism, white supremacy ideology and behavior, cultural imperialism, etc., we are a people who have survived because of our sense of community. Our readiness to help our sister or brother in need, to lend a hand while allowing another to regain or maintain a sense of dignity and self-worth has been the glue that has held us together. Nevertheless, in this age of "show me the money," we are in grave danger of making the mistakes that others have made, to ALL of our detriment and the detriment of the entire planet: placing things (money, materialism) before people. Money above relationships. Material acquisition above developing bonds of loving-kindness and mercy.

We are connected. Am I my brother's keeper? Of course I am. Because to ignore his pain, to ignore his lack, while accumulating my own abundance creates a breach that not only threatens my false security, but ensures the ultimate failure of us both, and us all.

Certainly hard cash is necessary. But, to what end? If I spend all my hard-earned dollars in black businesses that, in turn, do nothing toward the uplift of the larger community, whom have I profited? And what is the community but the people, individual lives and families, struggling for a sense of worth and dignity in the face of a larger reality that has historically, since the time of our enslavement, reduced us to dollars and cents?

There must be an element of "added value" in our concept of "buy black." Yes, we should support black-owned businesses with hard cash dollars. But even more importantly, if we are really serious about community development, we should be willing to support the individuals within our community who bring an abundance of creative gifts worth more than money. And by supporting our individual and collective talents and abilities, we develop and sustain the relationships that, no matter the unsettling and insecure times before us, have helped us to survive thus far, and will continue to see us through.

Will a model such as UMOJA Money community currency make us a formidable economic power to be reckoned with? Maybe, maybe not, in and of itself. It is very likely, though, that such a model will help strengthen and sustain us at our core, where it really matters. People helping people to attain and maintain a spirit of community, dignity and pride. Just how much is that worth to you?

GawaKazi or Shared Work

One way for a community to move gradually into the idea and implementation of community currency is the introduction to GawaKazi. GawaKazi is another way of contributing in a tangible manner to the life and spirit of the community.

Gawa is a KiSwahili term. Gawa meaning *"to share"* and Kazi means *"work."* GawaKazi is a unique community value-exchange enterprise which honors the unique gifts, talents and resources of all members of the community and provides the opportunity to share those gifts, talents and resources. It allows individuals and the community to place value on their skills, abilities and human resources, as well as provides an opportunity for intergenerational sharing. The sharing can include things such as tutoring, yard work, simple repairs, running errands, and storytelling. However, it is only limited by the human resources available within the community. GawaKazi is based on values that are in synch with the values inherent in indigenous communal societies, from Africa to Native American and throughout the world.

1. All members of the community are assets and have something to contribute.
2. Work is redefined to include any and all things that contribute to the overall health and wellbeing of the entire community.
3. Reciprocity is a community value that stresses "how can we help each other" versus "what do I get out of it?"
4. A network of people in any community working together is stronger and can achieve more than any one individual working alone.
5. Every human being matters, and should be treated with respect and dignity.

As part of orienting the community to this system of exchange, these values can be expressed and demonstrated.

This requires that individuals from the community be willing to offer something to each other – their neighbors, members of their faith communities, the elders, etc. Thus, one of the orientation activities might include having community members identify personal gifts and/or experience and to begin the process of making the commitments. The following survey may be helpful in that regard.

Gawa Kazi (Shared Work)
Skills Assessment Sample

Our community is blessed with an assortment of skills, talents, abilities and knowledge that we can build upon for the good of the entire community. The concept of GawaKazi (Shared Work) provides an opportunity for us to assess the skills available within our group, as well as those things that are need by other. With such an assessment completed, we can determine the best ways to swap and share those skills with each other. Some groups/communities utilize some type of "community money" or sharing coupons, whereby individuals who receive services can "pay" those delivering the services. Subsequently, those who receive the coupons may exchange them for goods and/or services that they may need.

For example, you bring me a small basket full of apples. I give you a coupon for designing/tying a resume. You don't need a resume but you do need someone to help you weed your garden. A neighbor, who is seeking work, volunteers to assist with the garden. As "payment," (if she agrees), is the coupon for help with a resume. She may then, in turn, cash in the coupon with me, in order to get the resume completed. Often we don't realize how many skills we actually have among us, never mind the types of services they can give and receive from other people that would help improve the lives of others. Frequently we take what we can do for granted and don't realize that something we do every day—driving, cooking, sewing, taking care of children and housecleaning, for example—could make a big difference in someone else's life. This survey also helps communities get a sense of what kinds of services are too expensive or hard to find within the community.

Please circle "give" for the things you can do and "receive" for the things you'd like to get from other people. If you'd like to both give *and* receive something, don't hesitate to circle both. Feel free to add to the list of you have gifts or needs that are not listed!

Health

Caring for the sick, elderly or disabled	Give	Receive
What did you do for them?		
Feeding and preparing special foods	Give	Receive
Bathing, grooming & dressing	Give	Receive
Companionship	Give	Receive
Fitness & Exercise: Yoga, Aerobics, Weight lifting	Give	Receive
Diet & Nutrition	Give	Receive
Massage & Complementary Therapies	Give	Receive
Mental Health Counseling	Give	Receive
Medical Services: Doctors, Chiropractors, Dentists	Give	Receive

Office & Professional

Typing, word processing, computer data entry	Give	Receive

Answering phones and taking messages	Give	Receive
Operating a switchboard	Give	Receive
Filing & keeping track of supplies	Give	Receive
Shorthand or speedwriting	Give	Receive
Writing business letters	Give	Receive
Bookkeeping	Give	Receive
Odd Jobs & running errands	Give	Receive
Operating a cash register	Give	Receive
Writing reports	Give	Receive
Managing other people	Give	Receive
Interviewing people	Give	Receive
Legal	Give	Receive
Product sales	Give	Receive
Telephone sales	Give	Receive
Door-to-door sales	Give	Receive

	Give	Receive
Security Guard or crowd control	Give	Receive
Home Maintenance & Repair		
Housecleaning:		
mopping, washing windows, vacuuming, dusting	Give	Receive
Garden & Lawn Care:		
Weeding, mowing, planting, pruning	Give	Receive
Plumbing:		
Fixing leaky faucets, unclogging drains	Give	Receive
Installing appliances, faucets, and fixtures	Give	Receive
Walls & Floors:		
Painting & wallpapering	Give	Receive
Knocking out walls	Give	Receive
Floor sanding or stripping	Give	Receive
Build room additions & install windows	Give	Receive
Install insulation	Give	Receive
Drywall & taping	Give	Receive
Install carpets	Give	Receive

	Give	Receive
Install wood floors	Give	Receive
Plastering	Give	Receive
Tile work	Give	Receive
Carpentry skills	Give	Receive
Cabinetmaking	Give	Receive
Roof repairs	Give	Receive
Electrical Repairs	Give	Receive
Appliance Repairs:		
Dishwashers, washers, dryers, refrigerators	Give	Receive
Bricklaying & Masonry	Give	Receive
Soldering & Welding	Give	Receive
Furniture Repair	Give	Receive
Installing/repairing heating & cooling system	Give	Receive
Repairing radios, TVs, VCRs, etc.	Give	Receive
Installing/repairing alarms or security systems	Give	Receive
Car maintenance	Give	Receive

	Give	Receive
Car repairs	Give	Receive
Food		
Baking		
Less than 10 people	Give	Receive
More than 10 people	Give	Receive
Preparing meals		
Less than 10 people	Give	Receive
More than 10 people	Give	Receive
Clearing/Setting tables		
Less than 10 people	Give	Receive
More than 10 people	Give	Receive
Washing Dishes		
Less than 10 people	Give	Receive
More than 10 people	Give	Receive
Bartending	Give	Receive

	Give	Receive
Catering	Give	Receive
Family Care		
Caring for babies under a year	Give	Receive
Caring for kids 1 to 6	Give	Receive
Caring for kids 7 to 13	Give	Receive
Working with teens	Give	Receive
Caring for elderly parents	Give	Receive
Taking groups of people on field trips	Give	Receive
Pet care	Give	Receive
Transportation		
Driving a car or van	Give	Receive
Driving a school bus	Give	Receive
Driving a taxi	Give	Receive
Delivery work	Give	Receive
Running errands	Give	Receive

Other

Sewing	Give	Receive
Upholstering	Give	Receive
Dressmaking and/or tailoring	Give	Receive
Knitting and/or crocheting	Give	Receive
House and furniture moving (and packing)	Give	Receive
Assisting in the classroom	Give	Receive
Hair dressing and/or cutting	Give	Receive
Doing phone surveys	Give	Receive
Music		
Singing	Give	Receive
Do you play an instrument? (Which one)	Give	Receive

Community

Have you ever organized or participated in any of the following community activities? Please check the ones that apply and write yes if you would like to participate in any of them again in the future.

Boy Scouts/Girl Scouts

Church or community organization fundraisers

Bingo

Rummage or yard sales

Church suppers

Parent-Teacher Organizations

Sports Teams – coaching or playing

Camping trips with kids

Field trips

Political campaigns

Community gardens

Neighborhood clean-ups

Community groups

Other groups or community work

Priority Skills

After going through the above list of different skills, please try answering the following questions.

- What three things do you think you do best?

- Are there any skills you'd like to teach?

- Are there any skills you'd like to learn?

"It is for the spring to give. It is for springwater to flow. But if the spring would continue to give, and the springwater continue flowing, the desert is no direction. Receiving, giving, giving, receiving, all that lives is twin. Whatever cannot give, whatever is ignorant of receiving, knowing only taking, that thing is past its own mere death. There is no beauty but in relationships. Nothing cut off by itself is beautiful. All beauty is in the creative purpose of our relationships." - Ayi Kwei Armah.

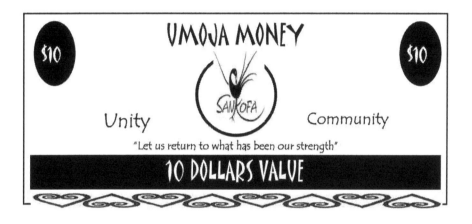